Traveling on the Freedom Machines of the Transportation Age

Thomas S. Owens

PERFECTION LEARNING®

With thanks to author Diana Star Helmer

Editorial Director: Susan C. Thies
Editor: Mary L. Bush

Cover Design: Michael A. Aspengren
Book Design: Emily J. Greazel, Deborah Lea Bell
Image Research: Lisa Lorimor, Emily J. Greazel

Photo Credits:
© CORBIS: pp. 4 (bottom), 10–11, 11, 21, 22, 26–27, 32; © Denver
Public Library, Western History Department: pp. 3 (bottom), 28–29,
34, 38; National Archives: p. 39

ArtToday (some images copyright www.arttoday.com):
cover (bottom-center, bottom-right), pp. 8, 16, 18–19, 31, 35; Corel:
pp. 4–5 (top); Library of Congress: cover (background, bottom-left),
pp. 1, 3 (top and center), 3 (bottom), 4 (bottom), 6, 9, 12–13,
15 (background), 17, 23, 25, 36, 37, 40 (background); Sue Cornelison:
pp. 14–15

For information, contact
Perfection Learning® Corporation
1000 North Second Avenue, P.O. Box 500
Logan, Iowa 51546-0500.
Phone: 1-800-831-4190
Fax: 1-800-543-2745
perfectionlearning.com

2 3 4 5 6 PP 08 07 06 05 04

Paperback ISBN 0-7891-5873-6
Reinforced Library Binding ISBN 0-7569-4490-2

Contents

Hoeing cotton and plowing fields were two jobs performed by slaves.

Chapter 1

Wheels Start Turning

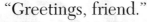

"Greetings, friend."

Joshua Chandler repeated the words over and over as he marched through a cornfield. He'd heard the words from Jacob many times. Now those words and thoughts of Jacob kept him company on this moonlit night.

Jacob and Joshua had worked Matthew Scott's fields together. Jacob had told Joshua many stories and taught him just about everything. Jacob was the only father Joshua had ever known.

Joshua had come to the Scott farm almost 12 years ago. Master Scott had bought him from the Chandler family farm. Master Chandler had given the young boy his last name to show ownership.

Two of the Scotts' slaves, Jacob and Mary, were given the child to raise until he was old enough to work. They'd chosen the name Joshua.

"You screamed all the color right out of you as a baby," Mary once said. "We don't know who your daddy was, but he must have been white. You're so pale, you could pass for a Scott baby. But don't you go repeating that," she warned.

"We don't look a thing like each other," Jacob had often told Joshua. "But to the Scotts, we just look like two slaves. And they never seem to notice that we're two slaves who do the work of ten!"

Then he'd squeeze the muscle in Joshua's small arm and laugh. "Of course, you do the work of one man. I do the work of the others!"

Jacob ran the Scott farm. Mary cooked and cleaned for the family in the Scotts' big house. Or at least she had—until last winter. One night in late December, Mary had died of a fever.

Then yesterday, on a bright spring day, Jacob had dropped

Female slaves were often responsible for household tasks such as cooking, cleaning, and doing the laundry.

dead guiding the plow. Joshua had buried him only hours ago.

He could still hear Jacob's voice in his head. "A runaway just has to listen," Jacob had whispered endlessly. "The helpers say 'Greetings, friend.' Then the slave knows he can trust the stranger."

Joshua had always wondered why Jacob and Mary hadn't tried to run away from the Scotts.

"Mary and I are as old as dirt," Jacob would say. "We're too tired to leave the only home we've ever known. We'll stay here until we die. But you, you're young. Someday your time will come."

Joshua knew that time was now. With Jacob and Mary gone, there was no reason to stay.

Besides, Jacob and Mary had always protected him from an angry master. He'd heard the yelling but had never seen the anger. Now, no one was left to protect him.

Would he need to do the work of three to satisfy Master Scott? Would he face three times the blame when things went wrong?

He had so many questions— and only one answer. He had to leave.

Arkansas was a slave state. He couldn't stay. He would follow the North Star to freedom.

Map of free and slave states and territories

WASHINGTON TERRITORY

OREGON

UNORGANIZED TERRITORY

MINNESOTA

MAINE

VERMONT

N.H.

NEBRASKA TERRITORY

WISCONSIN

NEW YORK

MASS.

CONN. R.I.

MICHIGAN

UTAH TERRITORY

IOWA

PENNSYLVANIA

N.J.

CALIFORNIA

ILLINOIS INDIANA OHIO

MARYLAND

KANSAS TERRITORY

MISSOURI

WEST VIRGINIA

VIRGINIA

KENTUCKY

NEW MEXICO TERRITORY

UNORGANIZED TERRITORY

TENNESSEE

NORTH CAROLINA

ARKANSAS

SOUTH CAROLINA

ALABAMA GEORGIA

TEXAS

MISSISSIPPI

LOUISIANA

FLORIDA

Free states and territories
Slave states

Conestoga wagons were sometimes called "camels of the prairie" because they carried heavy loads across the grassy lands (like camels in the desert).

Joshua slowed when daybreak arrived. Walking alone might invite a slave catcher. Had Master Scott put out a reward for him yet?

At the top of the hill, Joshua saw a wish on wheels—a Conestoga wagon. It wasn't a simple **buckboard**, a flat **platform rig** like Master Scott had. This wagon was as blue as the night sky. Its thick wheels could cut through the worst mud. The body was rounded a bit like a boat. An apple-red framework supported the wagon bottom. The white **canvas** roof made it look as though clouds covered the wagon.

Joshua ducked behind a tree trunk to admire the dream wagon. The four steam-snorting horses pulling the wagon stopped near the tree. Joshua thought about leaping to safety in the treetop. But before he could move, the wagon driver spoke.

"Greetings, friend!"

Joshua's mouth dropped open. "Pardon me, sir?"

The man had skin lighter than Master Scott's. But Master Scott had never smiled so warmly.

The driver laughed. "Yes, you heard me right. Friends will be waiting to greet you up North. But we must leave now."

Joshua needed only three bounces to land on the wagon seat. "I'm Joshua Chandler. I am, uh, I . . . Well, who are you?"

The driver smiled. "Do not question me, and I'll not lie to you. You may be safer not knowing your friends."

Joshua nodded slowly.

"Ya! Ya!" the driver called. The horses obeyed.

"I have apples in back," the driver said. "I sell my pickings to the riverboat travelers. I hope to do business in Memphis. Your future may rest on one of the steamships in **port** there."

Joshua nodded. Wagons. Steamships. How fast could he reach freedom? His mind was racing faster than any machine.

Friends and family await the arrival of a passenger steamship.

Chapter 2

Swimming Upstream

Joshua's smooth ride turned into a bumpy nightmare.

The whip cracked. The horses swerved. The wagon skidded off the road.

Suddenly the driver shoved Joshua off the seat. He tumbled into the back of the apple-filled wagon.

"Hey!" Joshua complained.

"Down and quiet, friend!" the driver hissed. His wagon glided into a **thicket** of trees. "We may have company."

Joshua bent down in the apple-sweet darkness. A minute or two passed in silence. Finally, the quiet coaxed him to peek out the back of the wagon cover.

The driver grabbed Joshua. He hurled the boy into a muddy **clearing**. Joshua struggled to his feet.

"Once more, please," the driver said. He shoved Joshua into the mud again.

When Joshua wiped the mud from his eyes and ears, he could see the stranger approaching.

"I am John Bush," the stranger growled. "Matthew Scott is missing a slave." Joshua saw the man on horseback tapping a pistol

Plantation police frequently stopped slaves to check their passes. A slave needed a pass from his master to leave the plantation.

$100 REWARD!

RANAWAY

From the undersigned, living on Current River, about twelve miles above Doniphan, in Ripley County, Mo., on 2nd of March, 1860, A NE GRO MAN, about 30 years old, weighs about 160 pounds; high forehead, with a scar on it; had on brown pants and coat very much worn, and an old black wool hat; shoes size No. 11.

The above reward will be given to any person who may apprehend this said negro ou. of the State ; and fifty dollars if apprehended in thi: State outside of Ripley county, or $25 if taken in Ripley county.

APOS TUCKER.

tucked in his belt. "Is this the runaway?"

The driver laughed. "I am Robert Welborn. This is my son, David. The boy wrestled a hornet's nest and lost. The mud eases his pain."

Joshua remained quiet, frozen in fear.

The **bounty hunter** boomed with laughter. "This bug wrestler doesn't look like any boy I seek. However, a reward is offered for the return of a slave boy. I can share such pay with anyone who helps my search. Good day, Mr. Welborn."

The driver waved at the retreating bounty hunter. Then he fetched Joshua from the mud. "Forgive me. You'll find a brook behind those bushes."

Joshua washed himself and his clothes. Then he crouched behind some bushes to wait. His mystery friend brought him apples to dine on in the bushy hideaway.

"I must go on alone," the man whispered into the bushes. "When your clothes are dry, dress and walk up the road to the hilltop. The Mississippi River awaits on the other side of the hill. We cannot speak again. Good luck, friend."

11

Joshua waved good-bye to the driver. He obeyed the orders and found another surprise over the hilltop.

"Houses on water!" he whispered in amazement. "Floating towns!"

Joshua knew no one could hear him. That didn't matter. He had to say it out loud to believe it. Each of the three steamboats was bigger than his master's house and barn together!

Joshua ran down the riverbank.

Still talking to himself, Joshua formed a plan. "The biggest will be best," he whispered. "More room to hide."

captains," he chuckled. "Someone has to pilot this fish north."

The word *north* tasted as sweet as a fresh apple to Joshua. North meant away from Master Scott. North meant no more backbreaking work. North meant freedom.

"And would you have a job for a strong young man to help you travel north today?" Joshua asked.

The captain frowned. He straightened his cap. "What are you running from?"

Joshua's eyes darted left and right. Then his face lit up. "Sir, you should ask me what I'm running *toward*. I've been waiting my whole life to be free—I mean, to be on my own. I want to see the world."

The captain smiled. "I understand. I got my own start from this very place when I was 12. I'll see what I can do for you."

Joshua dusted himself off and straightened his shoulders. He marched toward the uniformed man sitting on a tree stump smoking a corncob pipe.

"Good day, sir," Joshua began. "Are you in charge?"

A circle of smoke danced past Joshua. "That's what they tell us

Chapter 3

Feeding the Fire

Joshua shook hands with the pilot.

"I'm Captain Jerald Waterman," the man said. "That's my true name. A steamship pilot couldn't wish for a better one!"

Joshua introduced himself. In seconds, they made a deal and strolled aboard. Joshua wouldn't need a ticket for the ship. He'd pay for his travel by working.

Joshua's eyes widened as he looked at the top deck of the ship. Men wearing tall hats and shiny suits stood by the rail. Some laughed. One wound a gold watch. Another puffed a pipe twice the size of the captain's. Ladies' voices and laughter floated down to Joshua's ears.

Joshua's heart sank as he scanned the first deck. Beside a pile of wooden boxes was a line of men. They sat in a row, chained to a post.

The men were bigger and older than Joshua. Their skin was much darker. But they were slaves just like he was. No! Joshua wouldn't be a slave again. He'd do anything to stop that from happening.

Joshua felt the captain turn him sideways and push him through a door. Joshua cringed at the hot,

wet air. But the captain kept pushing him down the five stairs.

"Men, you have a new family member," the captain called. "Olaf. Hans. Meet Joshua Chandler."

Hans and Olaf nodded toward Joshua.

"Your job is easy," the captain promised Joshua. "Help the men feed the fire for our lady. She won't run if she doesn't have food. Now, I must get ready. We depart in 15 minutes."

Joshua thanked the captain. One of the men turned to him. Was it Hans or Olaf? Both men

looked alike. But in the fiery shadows, Joshua couldn't see anything clearly.

"My brother and I will teach you what to do." The man's words dipped up and down like a song. "First, you must not go on the deck. The captain hates passengers to see workers. We live down here."

The other brother nodded. "The boiler makes steam. The steam drives the engine. The engine turns the paddles through the water. It's like many men rowing with oars—but faster! But we must work now. We'll talk later."

Inside a boiler room

Joshua dragged firewood piles closer to the boiler. The air was wet and thick. He felt as if he were underwater.

Joshua looked at Hans and Olaf working without shirts. He removed his shirt too. Olaf handed him a rag. Joshua tied it around his head the way Mary had tied her handkerchief.

Hans smiled at Joshua as he manned the boiler door. His two bright eyes looked like a raccoon's mask in the middle of his soot-smeared face.

WHEEEEEEEEEE!

Joshua jumped at the sound. He groaned as a chunk of wood dropped on his foot.

"Ship whistle," Olaf said. "We're off!"

"Drink?" Hans asked Joshua. "There's a bucket over there."

Joshua took the dipper. One mouthful was enough. The water was hot and salty. Some soot chunks crunched between his teeth. Joshua spat. Both men were too busy to laugh at the newcomer.

Joshua staggered back to a woodpile. The door to the boiler room burst open. Joshua shaded his eyes from the shower of bright light.

"More power," the messenger barked. "We can't get upriver. Hurry!" The door slammed.

"Get those barrels!" Olaf ordered. "Over here. Fast!"

Joshua pushed, slid, and rolled the first wooden keg. Hans popped the lid.

"Candle wax?" Joshua asked.

"Close," Olaf said. "It's **resin**. It burns faster and hotter than wood. Adds more power."

The boiler gobbled up the resin like a starving child.

"Another!" Hans shouted.

Joshua obeyed. The fire roared.

Suddenly the brothers stopped. They stared at the boiler. Their eyes bulged. The boiler squealed.

"Get out!" Olaf shouted.

Hans picked up Joshua. The explosion hurled them through the doorway.

Chapter 4

Sink or Swim

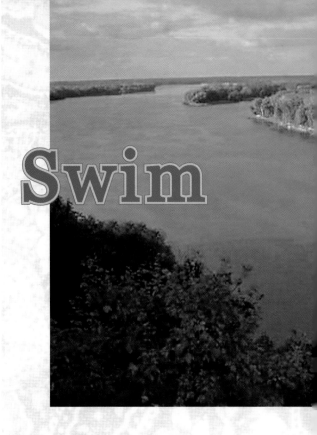

Joshua tried to wake up. Had it all been a dream—or a nightmare? He remembered flying through the air with Hans behind him. Where was Hans? And what about Olaf?

Joshua tapped his ears. They still rang and buzzed from the whoosh of the flames.

The ship wasn't moving forward anymore. It was tilting!

Joshua felt his ear again. When he looked at his hand, it was striped with blood. He felt the wound on his scalp.

Joshua covered the cut with the rag on his head. He had to find Hans and Olaf.

"Help is coming from shore. Please stay calm. The ship will stay afloat." The captain gave orders from the top deck. He shouted through a tube to make his voice louder.

People weren't listening. They were rushing off the ship. Joshua saw several small rowboats lowered over the rail. The fancy-dressed men and women shoved one another to get a seat on a boat to safety.

"Oh, no! Olaf! Why?"

Joshua turned. He saw Hans kneeling and wailing. Olaf was there too. But he was lying flat on his back, stretched out. He wasn't moving.

Joshua crawled across the swaying deck to reach the

brothers. "Hans, you saved me. Thank you!" Joshua said.

Then he looked at Olaf. "He's all right—isn't he?"

Pink stripes ran down Hans's sooty face. The stripes were painted by his tears. He shook his head.

"He saved us both. But he's gone. The blast got him. It will get us all. We will die in this evil river."

Joshua closed his eyes. He wanted to scream. He was too close to freedom to die now.

A dining table slid past on the deck, banging into the rail.

"Wait!" Joshua shouted. "That's our ticket to shore. Hans, turn the table over. Now!"

Hans didn't move. Joshua shook him by the shoulders.

"It will float like a raft," he yelled into Hans's face. "It will be our boat!"

Hans finally stood. He flipped the huge table without Joshua's help. They stretched Olaf's limp body onto the table. Grabbing two table legs, they lowered their craft into the water.

"It floats!" Hans shouted.

"Wait!" Joshua ordered. He skittered back across the deck. He spotted the shovel they had used to scoop ash. Joshua grabbed it, adding it to the table. He remembered digging Jacob's grave on the farm. How many graves would be needed today?

Both men floated beside the table. Each grabbed a leg for safety. Joshua saw suitcases bobbing in the water. He prayed there would be no more bodies in the river that day.

The swirling tides carried them to shore. Joshua refused to look back at the ship. They dragged Olaf's table to dry land.

"This is where we will bury him," Hans told Joshua.

They took turns with the shovel. Before placing Olaf in the grave, Hans checked his brother's pockets. He pulled out a small book. Then Hans nodded. Joshua said a prayer and then covered Olaf, scoop by scoop.

When he finally looked up, he saw Hans returning from the bushes. He had bound two sticks together to form a cross for his brother's grave. Hans knelt and said a prayer in a language Joshua didn't understand.

Joshua smiled at Hans. "He was a good man."

"And a good friend," Hans added. "We used to read to each other in the light of morning. This book is called *The Immigrant's Travel Guide*. We'd read and take turns dreaming of traveling across this great country."

Joshua blinked back tears. "Could you read it to me?"

Hans sighed. "In the book, steamboats are called 'flying palaces.' But we know differently now."

Joshua gulped. "Tell me more."

Hans laughed a tiny laugh. "The book warned us." He flipped to a page and then very slowly read aloud. " 'Traveling by steamboats is not without its dangers. Many accidents and lost lives are a result of the explosion, burning, or sinking of steamboats.' "

Hans stopped reading and looked at the sky. "We crossed that ocean. We laughed at the danger. We needed the work."

Joshua pointed to the book. "You could still find other ways to travel."

Hans squeezed the book as if he were squeezing his brother one last time. "I will stay here near my brother. I will work for a farmer nearby. Maybe I will own this land someday. My traveling days are over. It was meant to be."

Joshua stared at the grave. This fate may have been meant for Hans and Olaf, but not for him. His traveling days had just begun.

Chapter 5

Making Tracks

Joshua had begged Hans to read him the page about trains over and over. Now the words swam in Joshua's head.

" 'The railroad is a safe and speedy way to travel,' " Hans had read.

"Safe and speedy. Safe and speedy," Joshua repeated endlessly. The words clacked like the trains he'd heard but never seen at nights on the Scott farm.

Joshua nodded as he kept walking down the riverbank. He wanted to get far away from Captain Waterman's ship. He didn't want to know what had happened to it—or the people aboard.

He couldn't stay to farm with Hans. It wouldn't be safe. How far behind was John Bush? That man had hunter's eyes. He didn't need to shoot down what he hunted. He could stare it down.

Canal boats placed advertisements on their masts.

Before leaving, Joshua talked to Hans about his travel plans. Hans and his brother had been many places. They'd traveled in different ways.

Hans told Joshua about canal boats.

"A canal?" Joshua had interrupted. "Is that a river?"

"No," Hans said. "People dig smaller streams. They are like roads of water. Mules pull some of the boats. Each path has locks."

Joshua smiled. "To keep someone from stealing the water?"

Hans sighed. "A lock is a part of the path. Gates let more water in or out to raise or lower the boats."

Joshua stared at Hans. "Are canal boats faster than steamships?"

Hans snorted. "Not likely. The book says they are the safest but *slowest* way to travel. Olaf and I found that out quickly. They packed us in, shoulder to shoulder. We stood for the entire trip. No beds. No chairs. We were like apples in a barrel. By the time we finally arrived, we felt like applesauce."

So Joshua had focused on trains. Hans had read and read. Joshua had grown more and more excited—until the last sentence.

" 'Sometimes a train may run off its track, which may be out of repair in places. Occasionally explosions occur.' "

Joshua bit his lip. "Explosions? Like . . ."

"Like on the ship," Hans said, nodding.

Joshua preferred travel without explosion. But he'd never seen a train up close, and he couldn't help wanting to.

He only had a little experience with train tracks. One night, free men who put down train tracks had passed by the Scott farm. Mary and Jacob had sneaked them some cornbread. Jacob had called them *gandy dancers*. They sang strange, beautiful songs as they worked. Joshua had hummed their tunes for weeks after their visit.

Maybe *I* could be a gandy dancer, Joshua thought. But he didn't know anything about laying or fixing tracks.

Gandy dancers

Looking in all directions, he wished he had a map. He wished he could *read* a map if he had one. Actually, he just wished he could read anything.

Where were the towns? Joshua knew little about towns or states. Jacob had given him a lesson about maps and reading once. Joshua winced in pain as he remembered.

When Joshua was younger, he'd drawn marks in the dirt with a stick. He'd run to get Jacob.

"See? This mark is where we are. That mark up there is the next farm over," he'd pointed out proudly.

Jacob was silent. He backed Joshua into a tree trunk. Eyes narrowed, he pressed his nose against Joshua's.

"Don't you *ever* draw, read, write, or think map!" Jacob hissed. "If you do, Master Scott will beat you and all of us who know you. If he knows you even *think* of somewhere else, he'll think you will *run* somewhere else. A map-loving slave is a dead slave!"

Joshua's ears rang now, just as they'd rung when Jacob shoved him. No, wait—he really did hear ringing. A train whistle shrilled in the distance. Looking over the next hill, Joshua spotted a trail of smoke. He headed in that direction.

The walk took ages, but Joshua topped the hill at last. He saw tracks stretching across the valley. Two rows of gray steel with wooden middles ran between the hills. They reminded Joshua of a glowing, twisting ladder.

It was a railroad track. But the sound and the smoke—and the machine that had made it—were nowhere to be seen.

Then he spotted a building. It looked like a house or a barn. This must be where the travelers started or ended their trips. This was where he needed to be.

Chapter 6

Angel Wings

Joshua climbed onto the train **depot** platform as the sun was setting. He saw that the building was locked.

Huge wooden boxes sat on the platform. They were protected by the overhang of the depot's roof.

"Are you waiting for a train too?" Joshua asked the boxes. He was too tired to laugh. He knew

Jacob would have laughed though.

Joshua circled the building. Near the front door, he saw a water **trough**. He also noticed that some horses had ignored a snack of hay nearby.

"I think I've found a bed and bath!" Joshua exclaimed.

Once the safety of night came, he washed in the water. Then he took handfuls of hay and built a bed behind the boxes.

Joshua dreamed of his lost friends and family. All of them were sitting around an apple barrel. He was eating and laughing with Mary, Jacob, Mr. Welborn, Hans, and Olaf.

When he woke up, Joshua felt alone again. He couldn't see anything, but sounds surrounded him. Horse whinnies and loud voices filled the air.

He dusted off the bits of his hay bed. He tried to see what was going on without being noticed. He wanted to clean up first, so he would look like any other train traveler.

Finally, Joshua stepped into the sunlight and smiled. People of all ages buzzed about the depot like bees near a flower. Everyone had places to go and people to see. They had plans. They had futures.

Joshua's smile faded faster than yesterday's train whistle. Everything seemed to make sense for everyone else. Joshua blinked back tears.

Then he saw a smoke-burping steam train nearing. He glanced at the tracks. Surprised, he looked again. He pointed, but no one noticed. His mouth opened. He was too scared to scream.

Joshua leaped off the platform and ran down the tracks. He ran toward a young boy who had his back turned to the train. The boy was leaning down over the rails.

As the train approached, Joshua took one giant leap across the tracks. The two boys rolled together in the dirt seconds before the train passed.

"Not fair!" the freckle-faced, red-haired boy grunted. "I wanted to put a penny on the track so it would get squished flat."

Joshua stared at the boy in disbelief. "You were about to *become* that flat penny!"

A screaming woman flew at the boys. "Billy, my baby! My son!" Emily Buskirk sobbed.

Joshua stepped aside as the woman hugged and kissed Billy. Then she grabbed Joshua too. "Who are you?" she demanded.

"Joshua Chandler."

The lady shook her head. "No, you're not." She smiled through her tears. "You're an angel. You flew down and saved Billy!"

Embarrassed, Joshua pulled away. "Thank you," he mumbled and turned to go.

"Wait!" she blurted. The woman grabbed Joshua's hand. "Billy, let's ask your new friend to sit with us on the way to Chicago. Joshua, will your parents mind?"

Joshua's heart stopped. "I'll—I'll be meeting my family up North," he fibbed. "I was just about to buy my ticket."

The woman smoothed her hair. "Splendid. I insist on buying your ticket as a reward for your kind deed. And it will be a great load off my mind if you keep Billy company on the ride."

"My daddy's an architect," Billy piped. The big word sounded funny coming from a little boy's mouth. "He's been working on buildings in Chicago. We're going there to meet him."

In seconds, Mrs. Buskirk returned with the tickets. She motioned for Joshua and Billy to follow. The boys climbed up the two steps into what looked like the world's longest box on wheels.

"Do we stand in here?" Joshua asked.

"Oh, Billy. You have a funny friend," Mrs. Buskirk laughed. She opened a small door into a

room grander than the Scott family's parlor.

Joshua just stared at the lace curtains, wide windows, and soft leather seats. Joshua had never even imagined anything so fine.

A man wearing a white jacket and gloves closed the door. A screeching sound made Joshua jump. He pushed his feet hard against the floor as the train lurched forward.

"You don't get out much, do you?" Mrs. Buskirk asked kindly.

The train was moving. Joshua looked out the window. Houses, cornfields, and cows flew past his eyes. Billy babbled. Joshua nodded without speaking. He was too amazed at all he saw.

Joshua watched Mrs. Buskirk fumble with a small **satchel**. "Here they are! I have apples for everyone."

In the 1890s, companies competed with one another to create the most luxurious train cars.

Billy pinched his nose and waved away the fruit.

"Fine," Mrs. Buskirk said. "More for Joshua."

Billy grunted. "I wish you had fried chicken in that bag."

Joshua looked down so no one would see how fast he ate. One apple tastes like a whole fried chicken to a runaway slave, he thought. Especially when you've been running so fast, you haven't had time to eat.

"You ate the core!" Billy cried. "You're not supposed to eat that part!"

Joshua ignored him and kept eating. "Thank you," he sighed at last.

"You're welcome," Mrs. Buskirk replied. "I'll have another surprise for you when we get to Chicago tomorrow."

Joshua leaned forward. "What?"

Mrs. Buskirk rubbed her hands together and giggled. "I'll buy you a copy of the Chicago newspaper. Did you know that your name will be listed in all the Chicago papers? A list of arriving first-class train passengers is printed daily. The whole world will know where to find Mr. Joshua Chandler."

Oh, no! Joshua thought. Would that world include the bounty hunter John Bush?

Chapter 7

Free As a Bird

Joshua heard the train wheels grind.

"Welcome to Chicago!" the **conductor** called.

Joshua burst out of his seat. "Thank you," he called to a surprised Mrs. Buskirk.

Joshua charged down the crowded aisle of passengers. He shoved open the door of the cabin and bounded off the train's first step.

"Ooof!"

He hit something hard and reeled back. Two huge hands stopped him. The bounty hunter stared down at him.

"I'm John Bush," the man said. A tooth was missing from his evil grin. "Mr. Scott sent me. I read about your arrival in the newspaper. Quite helpful."

The hunter's eyes froze Joshua in place. "I have your papers. They prove that Mr. Scott paid for you," John Bush sneered. He blocked Joshua's path. "Your master will pay to get you back. I intend to collect the reward. Come quietly or—"

More than one horse had stepped on Joshua's foot when he'd tried to hitch them to a plow. Today, Joshua pulled the horse's trick. He ground his heel into the man's toes. The man let him loose with a howl.

Three steps away, Joshua spotted a strawberry-cheeked woman dressed in black.

"Auntie, help me!" Joshua shrieked. He threw his arms around the woman's waist and wailed.

"Please help me," Joshua whispered to the woman.

The woman began to pull away from Joshua. She stopped at the sight of the bounty hunter. Quickly, her eyes searched Joshua's.

"Sir, leave my nephew alone!" the woman barked.

John Bush wiped sweat from his face. "Step away from my property!" he hissed. "The boy belongs to me."

Joshua tried to take shelter behind the woman's full skirt. "You do not own my family," she corrected. "The people of this city will not stand for your behavior."

Train conductors took tickets, assisted passengers, and gave directions and signals to other train workers.

crouching boy. John Bush sprawled on the depot's **cobblestones**.

"Conductor, he bit me!" the bounty hunter huffed. "And she tried to kill me!"

The uniformed ticket taker tried to pick up the grunting man.

The woman batted her eyes. "Me? A lonely **widow**?" she asked. "How could I attack someone when I am filled with sadness?"

"Sir, I had dropped to my knees to pray," Joshua sniffled, still on his knees. "I thought Auntie and I would suffer at this man's evil hand."

Joshua forced a frown on his face. He raised his hands to the sky and squeaked, "Help us! My uncle has died. Spare us!"

The conductor didn't remove his hands from the bounty hunter.

John Bush flashed his yellow and brown teeth. He grabbed the woman by both shoulders. "I'll show you just how bad my behavior can be. You—ow!"

Joshua had dropped to the ground. He'd bitten the man's ankle as if it were a strip of bacon.

The sky darkened as Joshua felt a mountain topple over him.

The woman had shoved the wobbling bounty hunter over the

"Attacking a child and a woman," he snorted. "Bothering a family in mourning. The Chicago police will deal with the likes of you. Let's take a walk."

"No, you're wrong! You'll see! Boy, come back!" John Bush babbled as he was herded out of sight.

"Thank you," Joshua blurted and turned to run. He knew that standing still was a gift only free men could enjoy. And he wasn't free—not yet. He would never be free while he was still in America.

The woman clamped her hand on Joshua's shoulder. "You must stay!" she commanded.

"No, I can't." Joshua couldn't explain. There were too many people around. "Let me go. Please!"

"Shhh!" She held Joshua's shoulders and stared into his eyes again. *"Greetings, friend."*

Joshua stopped struggling. The woman straightened.

"Let's go now," she said. "Together."

Then the woman curtsied. No adult—white or black—had ever bowed to him. Joy bubbled like a steamship boiler inside Joshua.

But suddenly he wondered. "Have you truly lost your husband?"

She smiled half a smile. "You think I'd wear these sad rags only to fool the foolish?" she asked. Then she thrust out her hand. "Talking stops traveling," she scolded. "No more questions now. Let us reach Canada first. You'll be free as a bird there."

Joshua put his hand in hers. He knew he could trust her. He'd sailed across the water. He'd soared across the land. But at that moment, he felt as if his heart had wings.

Freedom Machines

In the 1850s, getting places in America was easier than ever. Never before had there been so many choices of ways to travel and places to go. It was the "Transportation Age."

Traveling on Roads

Roads weren't like the roads that travelers know today. Roads of the 1850s were rough and unpaved. A road might be interrupted by tree stumps or even farm fields!

The first major link between the East Coast and the Western frontier was the National Highway. Building began in 1806. The highway started in Cumberland, Maryland. It stretched 600 miles to Vandalia, Illinois.

The National Highway was a clear path from east to west. But like other early roads, it did not always offer smooth travel. Deep

Colorado Stage and Express Co.

Leaving Canon City at 7.30 a.m. daily, and arriving at Rosita and Silver Cliff at 3.00 p.m.

same day, making close connection both ways with the Denver & Rio Grande Railway.

RUNNING DAILY FROM CANON CITY
TO
SILVER CLIFF, ROSITA, ULA, COLFAX, AND DORA CITY.

Six Horse Concord Coaches.

THROUGH TICKETS FOR SALE AT DENVER AND PUEBLO.
LUTHER WELLS, Proprietor.

wagon-wheel ruts swallowed new carriages. Grooves carved by wheels became small swamps when filled with rain.

The broad wheels of the Conestoga wagon could handle the bad roads better than earlier wagons. The type of wagon Robert Welborn drove was named after the Pennsylvania valley where it was invented.

Use of the Conestoga wagon began in the East. The wagons were copied and used in other regions as their popularity spread. Conestoga wagons helped carry products before railroads. Being shaped like a boat kept the **cargo** from bouncing around the wagon as much.

Stagecoaches became another popular method of road transportation. Travelers would leave from a station or stop on the route. The space was shared with six to twelve people. Often these people were strangers who all wanted more room or a window seat.

The driver sat outside on top of the stage. Often a conductor sat nearby. He was in charge of the

Mark Twain

passengers and the cargo stored on the stage roof.

Stagecoach rest stops were fast and frequent. Horses were changed every ten miles. Four to six horses pulled one stagecoach. The best stagecoaches traveled 125 miles in a day.

In 1872, author Mark Twain described the stagecoach he used in a trip to California as a "cradle on wheels." Many travelers before and after Twain didn't agree. Although these coaches were covered and had a window, travelers weren't protected from extreme cold, heat, or dust. One bump could send a stagecoach passenger sprawling into a pile of other travelers.

Traveling by Water

In 1807, Robert Fulton's steamboat, the *Clermont*, made its first long trip from New York City to Albany, New York. Soon these ships became the fastest and most efficient means of travel.

Steamboats brought many dangers to the world of travel. The boilers for the steam engines made energy to turn the huge paddle wheels. Some ships tried fueling boilers with resin. Although resin burned faster than wood, the extra heat could create too much pressure in the boilers. This led to explosions, many of which killed passengers and crew.

Most steamboat dangers hid in the river water. Dead trees called *snags* lurked on or below the surface of the water. A steamboat pilot might not see the jagged wood hiding in the water until it was too late. Many steamboats sank due to snag collisions.

But despite the dangers, steamboats continued to be a popular method of transportation in the 1800s. Some were even used for fun. Famous steamboats raced against one another. The results were reported by newspapers as if they were professional sporting events.

Steamboat Show

Want to take a virtual tour of a steamboat? This site provides information on the parts of a steamboat and how they work.

http://www.steamboats.org/eexplore.htm

Traveling on the Rails

Another steam-powered machine played an important role in the Transportation Age. Steam locomotives, or trains, traveled at amazing speeds of up to 60 miles per hour. They could haul loads much larger and heavier than a team of horses could. The speed and efficiency of trains soon made them a very popular way to travel for both business and personal trips.

However, the introduction of trains to the travel era was not without problems. Many towns didn't have tracks running nearby. Some people had to travel far just to reach a train station.

Not all tracks were kept in good condition. This caused **derailments** and train wrecks. Sometimes, two trains heading toward each other would crash on one track. Other times, trees or cows blocked the paths of trains and caused accidents.

Sleeping on a train was too costly for many people. Seating wasn't always padded and roomy.

Meals were not served on most trains until the 1880s and 1890s.

Gandy dancers were groups of men who laid or repaired train tracks. The movements the men made while laying or fixing the tracks looked like dances. These men sang songs and chants as they worked. Each song had a specific meaning or went with a specific job. Some were coded messages that the workers understood but the bosses didn't. The songs helped the men accomplish difficult tasks and raised the spirits of tired workers.

Traveling to New Lives

Towns sprang up around train depots and river landings. Rivers were no longer seen as barriers separating people. Now the waterways were connections to speed people from one place to another. Businesses could make their products near rivers and easily ship those goods to customers. Hotels and restaurants were built for river businessmen and travelers.

As new ways of transportation became a part of American life, people sought information about these traveling machines. To meet this need, many books about the new travel choices were published in the 1850s. The book that Hans and Olaf read in the story was modeled after these books.

Like Joshua in the story, poor people had fewer choices in these new ways of travel. They could work on a train or boat. They could trade their services for transportation. However, workers were crowded into tiny spaces on ships and trains. They didn't enjoy the same fine food and comfort that paying passengers received. On the earliest steamboats, slaves would be chained together on the lower deck.

Wealthy travelers, on the other hand, enjoyed private rooms. They could dine or stroll on the upper deck. Sometimes, small bands would play on the top decks.

New forms of travel offered new jobs, homes, and adventures for many. For those like Joshua, travel offered freedom and new lives.

Glossary

bounty hunter person who hunts down and captures wanted people like slaves for a reward

buckboard four-wheeled wagon

canvas tightly woven cloth

cargo goods carried by a method of transportation (wagon, boat, train, etc.)

clearing area of land clear of trees or bushes

cobblestone naturally rounded stone used in paving streets

conductor person who leads or guides travel

depot building for railroad passengers

derailment a train leaving its tracks

platform rig wagon with a flat surface for hauling things

port place where ships dock to deliver or pick up goods

resin natural substance that burns easily

satchel small bag

thicket thick growth of small trees

trough long, shallow container that holds water for animals

widow woman whose husband has died